My William Shatner Man Crush

By

D. M. Larson

MY WILLIAM SHATNER MAN CRUSH BY D. M. LARSON

A full length comedy stage play script

3 males and 4 females with optional extras

Cast of Characters

Randy - a lazy roommate of Frank and Tony who is waiting for the perfect job

Frank - a cranky roommate of Randy and Tony who is a smart ass

Tony - the third roommate who is shy around woman and likes Jenny

Jenny - a friend of the three guys who likes one of them

Zora - an internet reporter who produces viral videos

Sadie - an elderly resident of a senior citizens home (can be played by Jane or any other cast member except Zora)

Jane - a protester who gets help from Tony (can be played by Sadie)

Reporter - radio voice (can be pre-recorded or played by another cast member)

Optional Extras - crowd (lines can be done off stage by other cast members if extras not available)

****

(ACT I takes place in the living room of an apartment. It's definitely the bachelor pad of a group of nerdy guys)

SCENE 1 - DEATH BY DOLLARS MONOLOGUE

                    RANDY
          Do you ever get winded putting on
          your shoes? That's me... I do. I'm
          fatty McFat Fat. I got super sized
          at Mickey D's, crowned at BK and
          supremed at the Bell. I am the all
          American consumer, consumed by
          convenience.

          I blame them... I do... They make
          it too easy... And cheap. That's
          me. Cheap and easy. I am a dollar
                    (MORE)

                                        (CONTINUED)

                         RANDY (cont'd)
          menu fanatic. I will eat anything
          for a buck. That's my motto.

          But is it death by dollars? I
          wonder if the dollar menus are
          killing me?

          But who can afford to eat right? I
          went in to one of them healthy
          places once. The cheapest thing in
          there was a grilled cheese sandwich
          and they wanted $5 for it! $5 for a
          grilled cheese!

          Maybe I could make super healthy pb
          and j's and sell them outside them
          ripoff restaurants...

(Calling out to invisible customers)
          Gourmet super healthy pbj for $4!

          And that $4 would get me a dollar
          menu feast.... Spicy chicken
          burger... fries... ice cold cola...
          and some pie. Dollar menu heaven.

          I'm getting kind of hungry. Gonna
          get me a spicy chicken sandwich
          while they last.

(Starts to rush but gets winded and grabs chest)
          If yesterday's $1 nuggets don't do
          me in on the way there.

                         END OF SCENE

SCENE 2

                         RANDY
          I wonder how long you have to work
          at KFC to become a colonel?

                         TONY
          Uh... you have to avoid any Major
          Messups?

                         RANDY
          Yeah... and enjoy corporal
          punishment?

                    TONY
And be a Captain of Industry.

                    FRANK
How goes the job hunting?

                    RANDY
Hey! They need someone to dress up
as a vegetable for a kid show.

                    FRANK
You know how to be a vegetable.

                    TONY
I thought you weren't allowed near
children.

                    RANDY
What I really want to do is be one
of those knights at that dinner
show where they do jousting and
such. That would be awesome.

                    FRANK
You with sharp pointy things? Is
that wise?

                    RANDY
Or a personal assistant for some
famous actor.

                    FRANK
I think your past history of
stalking celebrities might be a
problem.

                    RANDY
I wonder if William Shatner is
hiring.

                    TONY
Captain Kirk?

                    RANDY
That guy is awesome. I think he's
immortal or something. I don't
think he's aged since the 80's. I
can figure out his secret and write
a book about it or something.

                    TONY
Or something.

(CONTINUED)

                         FRANK
          Have you ever written anything in
          your life? I thought you always
          copied your reports in school.

                         RANDY
          I'm good at copying. Xerox is
          hiring.

                         TONY
          I'm not sure that's the kind of
          copying they specialize in.

                         FRANK
          Maybe you should go back to school.

                         RANDY
          I thought the principal said I
          couldn't come back... ever.

                         FRANK
          No... I mean college.

                         RANDY
          I heard Harvard was good.

                         TONY
          Um... maybe something a bit more...
          local... like a community college.

                         RANDY
          I'm tired of school. I did the 8th
          grade like 10 times. I'm so done
          with that.

(Randy finds something on his computer)

                         RANDY (CONT.)
          Look! Work from home. Be your own
          boss. This is perfect! Where's my
          phone?

                         FRANK
          That's a scam, Randy.

                         RANDY
          It says right here at the end. This
          is not a scam. I'm calling.
          1-900... I hate when they do words
          instead of numbers.

                    TONY
1-900-trick me?

                    FRANK
Really?

                    RANDY
Got it. It's
ringing. Hello? Yeah, I want to
do a home business and be my own
boss. What? A book? How
much? No thanks... I don't read.

                    TONY
At least he's honest.

                    RANDY
I can read... I just don't like to.

                    FRANK
So we need to find you a job that
doesn't involve reading and that
you can do from home.

                    TONY
A professional TV watcher?

                    RANDY
Yeah! They have that?

                    TONY
No.

                    RANDY
Way to get my hopes up.

                    FRANK
We have to find you something. Rent
is due...

                    TONY
His rent has been due for a few
months now.

                    FRANK
But he's working so hard with all
the chores he has been doing.

                    RANDY
What chores was I supposed to do
again?

                         TONY
               All of them.

                         RANDY
               Yes, master.

                         FRANK
               His lips say yes, but his butt says
               no.

                         RANDY
               Hey! Maybe I could do one of them
               fast food diets like Jared and the
               sandwiches... I'll do an all taco
               diet or something and then I can be
               in commercials and such.

                         TONY
               I don't think you'll lose weight
               eating tacos all the time.

                         RANDY
               I have to lose weight?

                         FRANK
               I'm thinking he didn't get the
               point of the whole Jared diet plan.

                         RANDY
               Why is everything so hard?

                         TONY
               Because you aren't able to live in
               your mom's basement like most guys
               in your situation.

                         RANDY
               What situation?

                         TONY
               Hmm... how do I say this nicely?

                         FRANK
               How do you tell someone they are a
               lazy bum without hurting their
               feelings?

                         RANDY
               Are you guys talking about me
               again?

                    TONY
          Maybe.

                    FRANK
          Yes.

                    RANDY
          Fine. You know what. I'm going to
          prove to you that I'm not lazy or a
          bum or a... no chore doer...
          don't-er or whatever. I'm gonna go
          out there and make something of
          myself.

(RANDY exits. FRANK and TONY go to the window)

                    TONY
          What's he doing?

                    FRANK
          When is the last time he went
          outside? I think the sun blinded
          him. He's waiting for his eyes to
          adjust.

                    TONY
          Does he even have a clue what he's
          doing out there?

                    FRANK
          I would bet money he forgot
          already.

                    TONY
          No... he's going... he took a few
          steps.

                    FRANK
          This is amazing... I'm getting all
          choked up. Our little boy is
          finally leaving the nest and going
          out in to the world all on his own.

                    TONY
          Nope... he's coming back.

(RANDY returns)

                    RANDY
          I forgot some stuff.

                         FRANK
              Like a resume?

                         TONY
              A plan?

                         RANDY
              My pro-wrestling mask.

                         FRANK
              Of course.

                         TONY
              Oh dear.

                         RANDY
              El Taco Feo lives!

(He puts on his wrestling mask and exits to fake cheering
that he produces)

                         FRANK
              Off to tackle the world.

                         TONY
              Or at least put it in a strangle
              hold.

SCENE 3 - A THING FOR NERDS

                         JENNY
              I've always had a thing for nerds.
              All kinds ... Geeky, Weirdo, Freak,
              Techie, Trekkie or Dork... you name
              it... I want to catch them all..
              Sorry for the Pokemon reference...
              I am a bit of a nerd myself. Girl
              nerds are rare but we do exist.

              I hung out with nerd-lings as a
              kid. We played Dungeons and Dragons
              and I loved being dungeon master
              ...holding their fates in my hands.
              It doesn't matter how pretty you
              are, just the fact you're female
              and like something nerdy makes you
              very attractive to them. Other
              kinds of guys could care less about
              me... But to nerds... I was hot.

              The more I hung out with boy nerds,
              the more I realized the power girls
                         (MORE)

                                                        (CONTINUED)

                    JENNY (cont'd)
have over them... There's nothing
they want more than First Contact
with the female of their species.

But with great power comes great
responsibility and I tried not to
take advantage... Much.

And the best thing about nerds is
that they give you their full
attention. Pretty boys are too
worried about their looks and
compete for the fairest of them
all... With pretty boys there is
always a fight for the mirror. With
tough guys and jocks... They always
want praise or worship. It's all
about them and they turn romance
into a competition ... (Does body
builder impression) Who is the
lucky girl who gets me today?

Nerds are the kindest kind of guy.
They have the best hearts... If you
get past the over drawn comic book
heroines and the overly aggressive
Sci Fi babes... They really care
about you and who you are.

You get a nerdy guy's full
attention. The rest of the world
slips away and you're his entire
universe, because no Death Star,
Tardis or warp drive is more
exciting than a girl who gives him
the time of day. That's why I like
these guys... I feel special...
important... and not alone anymore.

SCENE 4

(In comes Jenny)

                    JENNY
Hey guys. I saw loco Randy
wandering the streets in a
wrestling mask. Where's he off to?

                    TONY
We're still trying to figure that
out.

                                        (CONTINUED)

                    FRANK
          Either he's doing his taco diet
          idea or planning to be a
          professional wrestler.

                    JENNY
          Both seem likely scenarios for
          Randy.

                    TONY
          He's a dreamer.

                    JENNY
          Speaking of dreams, I had one about
          one of you last night.

                    FRANK
          Don't start, Jenny.

                    TONY
          Really?

                    JENNY
          It was pretty exciting.

                    FRANK
          Don't, Tony. It's a trap.

                    JENNY
          Come on, Frank. Play along. Please.

                    TONY
          I'm all ears. Tell me.

                    JENNY
          But Frank is taking all the fun out
          of it.

(Jenny sits all pouty)

                    TONY
          Frank. Be nice to our guest. Act
          curious or something.

                    FRANK
          I don't play games, Tony. I like it
          plain and simple. Either say what
          you got to say or don't say it at
          all.

                    JENNY
          Geez Frank. I see why you're
          single.

(CONTINUED)

                    FRANK
          I'm too busy building a career to
          get distracted by a relationship.

                    JENNY
          I didn't know working at BigMart
          was a career these days.

                    FRANK
          I'm advancing. I'm a manager.

                    JENNY
          Of the greeting card section.

                    FRANK
          And soon all of stationary will be
          mine.

                    JENNY
          Then on to ladies undergarments.

                    TONY
          In your dreams.

                    JENNY
          Speaking of which...

                    TONY
          Oh! Oh! Please tell me your dream
          was about me.

                    JENNY
          It was.

                    TONY
          Score!

                    JENNY
          But it was a little strange.

                    FRANK
          Here is comes and you walked right
          in to it, buddy.

                    JENNY
          We were alone...

                    TONY
          Shut up, Frank. I still want to
          hear this.

                    JENNY
          And it was dark...

                    TONY
          Yeah.

                    JENNY
          And you were a muppet.

                    TONY
          A muppet.

                    JENNY
          You know... like one of those
          puppet guys from Sesame Street.

                    TONY
          Like Cookie Monster.

                    JENNY
          Only way cuter... more like Oscar
          the Grouch.

                    FRANK
          He's cute?

                    JENNY
          I couldn't stop petting you.

                    TONY
          Really?

                    FRANK
          Here it comes.

                    JENNY
          But then I found out that some
          other guy was controlling you.

                    FRANK
          Oh no.

                    JENNY
          And he had his hand up...

                    TONY
          Never mind!

                    FRANK
          I told you, dude. You totally fell
          in to her trap.

                    JENNY
          He did. You do. Every time.

                    TONY
          She said she liked petting me. I
          had nice fur.

                    FRANK
          Only you could find something nice
          about all that.

                    JENNY
          He loves it when I torture him.

                    FRANK
          You're the perfect couple.

                    TONY
          We're a couple?

                    JENNY
          No.

                    TONY
          I mean, I wouldn't mind it if you
          wanted to go out or something.

                    JENNY
          I bet you wouldn't mind.

                    TONY
          Please, Jenny. Just one date.

                    JENNY
          Don't start begging. I hate that.

                    TONY
          I'll take you to your favorite
          restaurant.

                    JENNY
          Which is?

                    TONY
          The Leaning Tower of Pizza?

                    JENNY
          Maybe.

                    TONY
          And I'll take you to a movie... any
          movie you like.

                         JENNY
          And what kind of movies do I like?

                         TONY
          Superhero movies.

                         JENNY
          Maybe.

                         TONY
          And after, I'll take you to get
          dessert... your favorite.

                         JENNY
          Which is?

                         TONY
          Lemon margarine pie.

                         JENNY
          Wrong! You lose. No date. Thank you
          for playing.

                         TONY
          What? I can't believe this. What is
          your favorite dessert then?

                         JENNY
          That's for me to know and you to
          find out, big boy.

                         TONY
          Uh! I've got to go to work. I'm out
          of here.

(Tony exits)

                         JENNY
          That was fun.

                         FRANK
          Why do you torture him like that?

                         JENNY
          I torture all men. It's my mission
          in life.

                         FRANK
          That's not very nice.

                         JENNY
          This coming from one of the guys
          who like to go to the park and raid
          random people's picnics for food.

                    FRANK
          That's how we met you wasn't it?

                    JENNY
          I was not about to have my chicken
          stolen by three guys dressed as
          dorks.

                    FRANK
          Orcs.

                    JENNY
          Whatever.

                    FRANK
          We only do that on July 29 to
          celebrate the publication of Lord
          of the Rings.

                    JENNY
          Whatever squared.

                    FRANK
          And we've been stuck with you ever
          since.

                    JENNY
          We live in the same apartment
          complex. And I think one of you is
          cute.

                    FRANK
          Oh, no. Not this again.

                    JENNY
          You're not the least bit curious
          which one of you is a cutie?

                    FRANK
          Begone foul wench.

                    JENNY
          I've been called worse.

                    FRANK
          I bet you have.

                    JENNY
          Why are you so mean to me?

                    FRANK
          I'm mean to everyone.

(CONTINUED)

                         JENNY
          I've noticed. But why?

                         FRANK
          I don't know. I've just been in a
          bad mood most of my life.

                         JENNY
          Working at BigMart will do that to
          a guy.

                         FRANK
          At least I have a job.

                         JENNY
          I'm going to college.

                         FRANK
          For how many years?

                         JENNY
          Maybe I'm studying to be a doctor
          or lawyer or something.

                         FRANK
          Or maybe it's just taking you a
          really long time.

                         JENNY
          I've changed majors a few times.

                         FRANK
          A lot of times.

                         JENNY
          Only once a semester.

                         FRANK
          What is it now?

                         JENNY
          Philosophy... I think.

(Frank's phone rings. He answers it)

                         FRANK
          Hello.

                         JENNY
          Hi, Frank. This is your mommy.

                         FRANK
          Yes, this is Frank Ferrer.

                         JENNY
          I know, Frank. I gave birth to you
          remember.

                         FRANK
          What? Really?

                         JENNY
          Yes, I am your mother, Frank. I
          know because I was there.

                         FRANK
          How?

                         JENNY
          Are you ready for the birds and the
          bees talk now?

                         FRANK
          You have to be kidding me.

                         JENNY
          I know I should have had this talk
          with you sooner, but you didn't
          seem ready. But now that Jenny has
          been hanging around you, I suspect
          there are things you need to know.

                         FRANK
          Yes, I'm on my way.

(Frank hangs up)

                         JENNY
          What's up?

                         FRANK
          You are really obnoxious.

                         JENNY
          I know.

                         FRANK
          Guess who's in the hospital?

                         JENNY
          Randy.

                        FRANK
         Of course.

                        JENNY
         What happened?

                        FRANK
         I'm not exactly sure... they said
         he was playing superhero or
         something.

                        JENNY
         I wonder if he got super powers?

                        FRANK
         Gee, I wonder. Let's hurry to the
         hospital and find out.

                        JENNY
         Okay!

(They exit)

                    END OF SCENE

ACT II

(This scene continues in their apartment)

SCENE 5 - STEAM TRAIN MONOLOGUE

                        ZORA
         Do you ever feel like you're stuck
         on the front of a steam train going
         a million miles an hour?

         Flying down the tracks... so out of
         control. One slip and you'll be
         crushed into a million billion
         pieces.

         The pressure... Incredible pressure
         ...your chest pounding so hard your
         heart wants to break free....

         But you feel a little thrill don't
         you? And you realize it's better
         than the nothingness of your life
         before.

         Is it true? What kills you makes
         you feel alive?

                                              (CONTINUED)

Suddenly you realize this could be
the most exciting moment in your
life... Flying free down the
tracks... An adventure... No clue
where you're going or if you'll
survive ...but you're living.
Really living.

Is that why those stars do that...
Do something dangerous and
wonderful... So explosive... that
it will eventually destroy them...
Marilyn Monroe, Elvis, Michael
Jackson, Robin Williams... Riding
the steam train to their death...
Screaming with life?

There's no turning back... No
middle ground. Once you live...
really live... there's no way to go
back again. No brakes or safety
nets... No getting off the runaway
train.

So instead of being afraid, instead
of seeing it as an end to life...
You scream...

Bring it on steam train! ... Make
me live!

SCENE 6

(Randy is moaning as Jenny and Frank help him to the couch)

            FRANK
Could you go any more limp, Randy?

            RANDY
I can try.

            FRANK
That was sarcasm.

            JENNY
Be nice, Frank. Randy is in a lot
of pain.

            FRANK
He's a lot of pain all right.

(CONTINUED)

                    RANDY
          Oh!

                    JENNY
          What is it, Randy? What hurts?

                    RANDY
          Everything.

                    JENNY
          What can I get you?

                    RANDY
          I don't know...

                    JENNY
          Anything, Randy. Come on.

                    RANDY
          Maybe some cheetos, m and m's and a
          smoothie?

                    JENNY
          Uh... okay.

                    RANDY
          Smoothie recipes are on the
          fridge. I like the peanut butter
          chocolate one.

                    JENNY
          That sounds healthy.

                    RANDY
          Oh!

                    JENNY
          Okay, okay. I'll hurry.

(Jenny rushes to kitchen)

                    FRANK
          Look at you... Mr. Patient. All
          hurt and needing a nurse. If Jenny
          didn't deserve a little scamming,
          I'd call your bluff right now.

                    RANDY
          Why you being so mean, Frank? I'm
          really hurt. The hospital said so.

                    FRANK
          They said you might bruise and hurt
          a bit but nothing is broken.

                    RANDY
          Then why does it hurt so much?

                    FRANK
          Yes... why indeed.

(The sounds of a blender is heard)

                    RANDY
          She's fast. She's such a good
          friend.

                    FRANK
          You're lucky I don't kick you out
          of this apartment right now. Don't
          push your luck.

                    RANDY
          Oh!

(Randy is in pain and Jenny rushes in with all the requested
items)

                    JENNY
          Here you go, sweetie.

                    FRANK
          Sweetie?

                    JENNY
          I got you a straw for your smoothie
          so you don't have to sit up to
          drink it.

(In his best, hurty voice)

                    RANDY
          Thank... you...

                    JENNY
          Anything else?

                    RANDY
          Radio please?

                    JENNY
          He said please. That's so cute.

                              FRANK
                    Oh, please.

                              RANDY
                    87.8 FM please.

                              JENNY
                    Uh... okay.

                              FRANK
                    The news channel?

(Jenny turns on the radio - Announcer can be pre-recorded or
have the actor who plays Tony do it if an extra actor is not
available)

                              ANNOUNCER
                    Today in local news, a hometown
                    hero lands in the hospital after
                    attempting to rescue a bus full of
                    senior citizens.

                              RANDY
                    Oh! Oh! It's my story!

(Dramatic news music. Frank gives him a dirty look and Randy
gets in pain again)

                              RANDY (CONT.)
                    Oh! My... story.

                              JENNY
                    Really? It's about you?

                              ANNOUNCER
                    A masked man jumped in to action as
                    a bus full of senior citizens lost
                    control. The bus lost control when
                    the 30 year old driver suffered a
                    heart attack. A man wearing a
                    wrestling mask jumped on to the
                    runaway bus. We interviewed a
                    witness.

                              WITNESS (RANDY)
                    That bus was rolling down a hill at
                    about a gazillion miles an
                    hour. Then I saw the masked
                    wrestler hero guy jump out of
                    nowhere and leap on to the bus.

                                                    (CONTINUED)

                    FRANK
          Wait a minute...

                    JENNY
          Shhh!

                    ANNOUNCER
          Everyone on the bus was safe
          including the driver who is
          recovering in the hospital. If
          anyone has information on the
          identity of this masked hero, call
          us at 555-8787 now.

(Randy turns down the radio)

                    RANDY
          Where's my phone?

                    JENNY
          Were you the masked hero, Randy?

                    FRANK
          And the witness.

                    RANDY
          I can borrow your phone, Jenny? I
          think I lost mine when I jumped on
          that bus.

                    JENNY
          So that's how you got hurt? Saving
          all those old people?

                    RANDY
          Yes... I walking along, in my
          wrestling mask, trying to figure
          out what I might do for a job. I
          thought maybe I could be one of
          those guys the famous wrestlers
          warm up on or maybe I could be a
          guy that stands on a street corner.

                    FRANK
          On a street corner?

                    RANDY
          You know with a sign, for a Mexican
          restaurant.

                    FRANK
          Hey, that's actually not a bad
          idea.

                         RANDY
          Really? I thought the wrestling
          idea was my best bet.

                         JENNY
          What about the bus?

                         RANDY
          Well, I see this bus rolling out in
          to the street out of the senior
          citizen center and I think...
          whoa... they're in trouble so I ran
          for the door. It was closed so I
          ran in to it. The driver looked
          really scared... that must be
          because he was having the heart
          attack.

                         FRANK
          Or you caused it.

                         JENNY
          Let him tell his story, Frank.

                         RANDY
          And the bus driver fell out of his
          chair... he wasn't wearing a seat
          belt! Can you believe that?

                         FRANK
          It's hard to believe any of this.

                         RANDY
          Then I used all my strength to rip
          open the door, jumped inside and
          put on the break.

                         JENNY
          Amazing! You are a hero!

                         ANNOUNCER
          This just in...

                         RANDY
          Turn the radio back up.

                         ANNOUNCER
          A cell phone was found at the scene
          of the bus rescue. Authorities
          believe it might belong to the
          masked hero and are working to
          identify the owner of the phone.

          (Frank turns down the radio and looks at Randy)

                         FRANK
          Wow, it's like you planned this and
          left a clue.

                         JENNY
          I don't think Randy had this all
          planned out.

                         FRANK
          Probably not at first.

                         JENNY
          You really think Randy has the
          brain power to come up with such an
          elaborate scheme?

                         RANDY
          Yeah... thanks, Jenny.

                         FRANK
          Maybe Randy is the most brilliant
          person in this room. He doesn't
          work, he doesn't pay rent, he has
          you waiting on him... he's an evil
          genius.

                         RANDY
          Is he being mean? I can't tell.

                         JENNY
          If Frank is talking, he's being
          mean.

                         ANNOUNCER
          This just in...

                         RANDY
          Turn it up.

(Jenny turns up the radio again)

                         ANNOUNCER
          The authorities have identified the
          owner of the cell phone found at
          the scene of the senior citizen bus
          rescue. The owner of the phone
          denies being the masked hero
          although we suspect he is trying to
          protect his secret identity.

(Randy turns down the radio)

                    FRANK
          That's too good. It was someone
          else's phone.

                    RANDY
          I wonder if I took Tony's phone
          with me?

                    JENNY
          Oh, no. If it was Tony's phone...

                    FRANK
          They'll think he was the masked
          hero. That's too funny.

                    RANDY
          No, it's not.

                    FRANK
          Evil plan failed on you eh?

                    JENNY
          What's wrong with wanting to be a
          hero and help people?

                    FRANK
          Because I don't think that's why he
          did it.

                    JENNY
          Why do you always have to look at
          the dark side of everything?

                    FRANK
          We're talking about a guy who never
          helps anyone. He won't even do the
          dishes. The most heroic thing he's
          ever done is finish a hero
          sandwich.

                    RANDY
          A hero sandwich does sound good
          right now. Could you get me one,
          Jenny?

                    JENNY
          Sure, Randy. I'll get you one right
          now. Don't let this big bully be
          mean to you while I'm gone. I
          wouldn't want anyone to pick on my
          little hero.

(CONTINUED)

                    FRANK
          He's not a hero. Stop that.

                    JENNY
          I'm going to get his sandwich.

                    FRANK
          Can you get me one too?

                    JENNY
          No.

                    FRANK
          Why am I the one who is the bad guy
          here? I don't get it.

                    JENNY
          And you ain't never gonna get it
          either?

                    FRANK
          What does that mean?

(Jenny opens the door and is shocked at what she
sees. Frank comes and looks)

                    JENNY
          What's going on?

                    FRANK
          What's with all the reporters?

(Randy looks now too)

                    RANDY
          Are they here to see me?

                    FRANK
          No... they're chasing Tony.

(Tony rushes in)

                    TONY
          Shut the door!

(They do)

                    JENNY
          What's going on?

                    TONY
          They think that I'm some kind of
          hero who saved a bunch of senior
                    (MORE)

> TONY (cont'd)
> citizens on a bus. They found my
> cell phone on there. Randy... did
> you take my phone by mistake again?

> RANDY
> Maybe.

> TONY
> Now they think I'm some guy in a
> wrestling mask that was trying to
> be a hero.

(Frank holds up Randy's wrestling mask)

> TONY (CONT.)
> Wait a minute. Was that you, Randy?
> You were the... hero.

(Tony laughs when he says the word hero. Frank laughs with
him)

> FRANK
> Hee hee... I know. Crazy.

> JENNY
> You two stop being such jerks.
> You're hurting Randy's feelings.

(Jenny comforts Randy who is making a very hurt face. Frank
and Tony look a moment and then laugh even harder. There is
a knock at the door)

> RANDY
> It's the reporters.

> TONY
> They're all yours, buddy. Go have
> your moment in the sun.

> FRANK
> You sure that's wise?

> TONY
> He can have it. I got a taste of
> the press on the way home. I can
> live without ever seeing another
> reporter again.

(Randy opens the door and a beautiful reporter named Zora
walks in)

                         ZORA
          Which one of you is Tony Hawking?

(Randy raises his hand excited)

                         RANDY
          I am.

(Frank grabs Randy's arm)

                         FRANK
          You are not. He is.

(Tony weakly does a little wave. He is nervous)

                         ZORA
          So are you the hero I've been
          looking for?

(Tony gets even more nervous as he gets closer)

                         TONY
          I... well... uh...

                         RANDY
          Well, actually...

(Randy puts on the wrestling mask. Frank pulls it off and
tosses it outside)

                         RANDY
          Hey!

(Randy runs outside and Frank shuts the door on him)

                         TONY
          Oh, I'm no hero.

                         ZORA
          So humble... people will love that
          about you.

                         TONY
          Uh... really... I mean...

                         ZORA
          Can I interview you about this bus
          rescue? Come sit with me over
          here.

(She sits on the couch and Tony sits at the opposite end as
far as possible. Zora moves closer to him. Jenny sits in
between them)

                         JENNY
          So... what kind of reporter are you
          anyway?

                         ZORA
          What do you mean?

                         JENNY
          TV, newspaper, magazine?

                         ZORA
          Online. I have a blog and website
          called Heroes Among Us.

                         FRANK
          Oh, hey. I've seen that. You dress
          up in all kind of cool costumes.

                         JENNY
          Figures that's all you'd remember
          about it.

                         TONY
          I read it for the articles.

                         JENNY
          Sure, you do.

(Jenny gets up annoyed)

                         FRANK
          So you want to feature Tony?

(Frank sits on the other side of her as she scoots closer to
Tony)

                         ZORA
          I want to feature the masked hero
          who saved all those senior
          citizens. I want to do a featured
          story and a photo shoot.

                         FRANK
          Photo shoot... where you dress up
          like a super hero? Can he pick
          which one?

                         JENNY
          Ew.

                         ZORA
          I thought I'd dress as a damsel in
          distress in this one.

                                                    (CONTINUED)

                         JENNY
              Like one of the little old ladies
              he rescued. Grannie panties would
              suit you.

(Everyone ignores Jenny)

                         ZORA
              Was that you Tony? Are you the
              masked hero?

(Frank is nodding yes. Jenny gives him a killer look. Tony
isn't sure what to say as he stares at Zora and then he
sighs)

                         TONY
              No, it wasn't me.

(Zora suddenly stops being friendly and becomes more
reporter like again)

                         ZORA
              Then who was it?

(She looks at Frank who nods. Jenny smacks him in the head)

                         JENNY
              It was Randy.

                         ZORA
              Who?

                         JENNY
              The guy who ran out the door after
              his wrestling mask. You're a very
              observant reporter.

(Jenny opens the door and comes in with his mask on)

                         RANDY
              Farewell for now good
              citizens! Your hero needs to visit
              the crapper!

(Jenny shuts the door and Randy sees Zora. Randy stands all
heroic)

                         RANDY (CONT.)
              Is it me you seek?

                         ZORA
              Yes, so you're the hero who saved
              all those elderly people in
              distress.

                                              (CONTINUED)

                         RANDY
          It be I you need talk to.

                         FRANK
          He makes bad grammar sound so good.

                         ZORA
          Is there somewhere a little more
          private we can talk?

                         RANDY
          Let's see... my bedroom perhaps.

                         ZORA
          That would be perfect.

(Zora and Randy exit to his bedroom. Jenny mocks her)

                         JENNY
          "That would be perfect."

                         TONY
          She should have said it like
          Catwoman... "That would be
          purrr-fect."

                         JENNY
          She does reek of villain.

                         FRANK
          I think that breaks the record for
          how quickly any of us has gotten a
          woman in to his bedroom.

                         JENNY
          What was the previous record?

                         FRANK
          Uh... two years.

                         JENNY
          That quickly?

                         FRANK
          She really wanted to see my limited
          edition Avengers poster. She had a
          thing for Loki.

                         JENNY
          He is a hotty.

                    TONY
          Really? Yuck. I have no what
          women see in him.

                    JENNY
          Well, that's good. I'd be worried
          if you did understand.

                    FRANK
          So you want to see my poster?

                    JENNY
          I've seen the abyss you call your
          bedroom. I don't want to get
          trapped in there like she did.

                    TONY
          She got out... eventually.

(Tony does an evil laugh)

                    JENNY
          Oooo, that's good. Do it again?

                    TONY
          Mwhahaha!

                    JENNY
          Ooooo... you gave me
          chills. Again?

                    FRANK
          Knock it off, hyenas, and help me
          figure out what we're going to do
          with Randy.

                    JENNY
          What do you mean?

                    FRANK
          He's a big fat liar. I seriously
          doubt he saved anyone.

                    TONY
          It does seem unlikely.

                    FRANK
          I'm going to the senior citizen
          center and ask some questions.

                    JENNY
          Why bother? What's wrong with
          letting Randy have his moment in
          the sun?

                         FRANK
          Remember Comic Con and the Borg
          incident, Tony?

                         TONY
          Oh yeah. That's right. I forgot
          about that.

                         JENNY
          What happened?

                         FRANK
          Randy won a contest to get a Star
          Trek makeover at Comic Con. He got
          transformed in to a Borg on stage
          in front of a huge audience. And
          then he spent the rest of the day
          going around and doing a robot
          dance for everyone. He acted like
          he was a big deal and for some
          reason everyone believed he was
          some kind of celebrity. He really
          went crazy over it. He refused to
          take off the makeup at the end of
          the day and the studio people had
          to get security to hunt him
          down. He made a big scene at the
          Star Trek event that night and
          climbed up on to this huge
          promotional display. They had to
          get the Borg queen to talk him
          down.

                         JENNY
          So in other words, he gets a little
          crazy with too much attention.

                         TONY
          Bingo.

                         FRANK
          Speaking of bingo, I'm going to
          chat with some of elderly folks
          over at the senior center.

                         JENNY
          If any of those guys are as hot as
          William Shatner, get their number
          for me okay?

                         FRANK
          That's not gonna happen. Shatner
          is one of kind.

                                           (CONTINUED)

(Frank exits)

                    TONY
          Well, Jenny. Looks likes it's just
          you and me... alone... together.

                    JENNY
          And now it's just you... alone...
          bye bye.

(Jenny exits. Tony's head drops sadly and he sits on the
couch sadly. He discovers he sat on something. It's a comic
book)

                    TONY
          Well, hello Supergirl. Here to save
          the day?

                    END OF SCENE

SCENE 7 - MASKED MAN

(Zora is interviewing an old lady named Sadie at the senior
citizen's center which is a spotlight on stage)

                    SADIE
          Oh, it was so exciting. It reminded
          me of my senior prom... Or was it
          the time the bank was robbed?
          Either way, it was so exciting.

          I have always loved masked men. I
          enjoy a bit of mystery. Most men
          are so simple.... Easy to read. But
          a masked man becomes a whole new
          kind of man. One with something to
          hide. A mystery I must uncover.

          I miss Roger. He was a mystery. We
          met one of those costume parties
          where everyone was wearing a mask.
          It was his eyes... His beautiful
          eyes... I could get lost in those
          eyes forever. I never told anyone
          this but I know Roger was the one
          who robbed that bank. I recognized
          his eyes. And the way he waved that
          gun around and yelled at people...
          It was so scary... And exciting.
          That's always how he was.... Scary
          and exciting.

                    (MORE)

                                          (CONTINUED)

                         SADIE (cont'd)
It was so nice seeing Roger
again... Rushing on the bus, being
a hero. I like him being a hero
too. As long as he is in a mask. I
love the mask. Good or bad, the
mask is perfect.

Please tell him I'm here. That I
want to see him again... and give
him a kiss.

SCENE 8

(Randy enters upset)

                         RANDY
I don't want to talk about it.

(Randy rushes off to his room)

                         FRANK
When he walks in a room and says
something like that then I want to
talk about it.

                         TONY
I bet Zora dumped him.

                         JENNY
Were they dating?

                         FRANK
In Randy's head they were... she
probably just shattered his
reality.

                         JENNY
How sad.

                         TONY
I wish I'd seen it.

                         JENNY
You two are so mean.

                         TONY
I mean, I wanted to be there so
Randy had a shoulder to cry on...
and a wing man... I'd have his
back.

                    JENNY
          I so know you don't mean it.

                    FRANK
          Here comes trouble.

                    JENNY
          Zora?

                    FRANK
          Let her in... she's grinning.

(Tony opens the door for her. Zora comes in happily with a
tablet)

                    ZORA
          You all have to see this.

                    FRANK
          What happened?

                    ZORA
          It's too good. It's already gone
          viral.

                    FRANK
          Randy always has some virus or
          another.

                    TONY
          Viral video? Really? With Randy?

(Zora plays it for them. Jenny doesn't want near Zora so
Frank and Tony give her a play by play)

                    FRANK
          It's the senior citizen center.

                    TONY
          Randy is in his mask.

                    FRANK
          Look at that old lady move!

                    TONY
          She's jumping in his arms!

                    FRANK
          Wow! What a kiss!

(Jenny can't stand it and takes the tablet from them. She
can't help but laugh. They crowd around)

                         RANDY
              Who let her in here?!

(They all stop. Jenny gives Zora her tablet back.

                         RANDY (CONT.)
              What is that? The video! I can't
              believe this. Take that off
              YouTube right now!

                         ZORA
              No way. You signed an agreement.
              This video is staying. Plus it's a
              hit!

                         RANDY
              I'm so glad I'm wearing a mask.

                         JENNY
              What's happened? Why'd she do
              that?

                         RANDY
              She thought I was her long lost
              husband or love or something come
              back for her.

                         ZORA
              I thought it was kind of sweet
              actually.

                         RANDY
              Sweet?! You ever kissed an old
              person? French style? I have the
              weirdest taste in my mouth
              now. I'm brushing my teeth.

                         FRANK
              Do you own a toothbrush?

(Randy exits)

                         TONY
              I don't think so. Don't use mine!

                         JENNY
              So you're leaving that video
              online?

                         ZORA
              Of course.

(CONTINUED)

                    JENNY
That's terrible to exploit people
like that.

                    ZORA
Exploiting people is what news is
all about.

                    JENNY
And you love every minute of it.

                    ZORA
I do.

                    JENNY
Get out.

                    ZORA
What?

                    JENNY
Get out before I scratch your eyes
out.

                    ZORA
Do you even live here?

                    FRANK
You better go, Zora.

                    ZORA
I don't think Randy wants me to go.

(Randy comes out brushing his teeth. Speaks while brushing.
This makes him foam at the mouth)

                    RANDY
Yes, I do. Bye bye.

                    JENNY
You heard the man... bye bye.

                    ZORA
I'll be back.

                    JENNY
We'll be ready.

                    ZORA
Whatever.

(Zora exits. Tony goes over to Randy)

                    TONY
          That's my toothbrush!

                    JENNY
          Spiderman?

(Randy holds it out to him)

                    TONY
          Keep it.

(Randy shrugs and puts it in his back pocket)

                    RANDY
          Thanks for backing me up, Jenny.

                    JENNY
          I'm awesome like that.

                    TONY
          Yeah.

                    JENNY
          I can't believe she did that to
          you. Did you really sign something
          giving her the right to film
          everything and keep it.

                    RANDY
          She asked for my autograph... it
          was at the bottom of a paper with a
          lot of writing on it.

                    FRANK
          And you didn't read it.

                    RANDY
          Reading is hard.

                    FRANK
          Wow... you're really special Randy.

                    RANDY
          Thanks.

                    TONY
          Can't we flag the video or
          something?

                    FRANK
          It's worth a try. I'll see what I
          can do. Come on, Randy. Let's try
          to get rid of that video.

(Frank and Randy exit)

                    TONY
          That's pretty cool how you stood up
          to Zora.

                    JENNY
          She's a bully. I hate bullies.

                    TONY
          Aren't you worried bullies will...
          bully you or something?

                    JENNY
          Most of the time they back down. A
          lot of them are all bark and no
          bite.

                    TONY
          But what if they aren't?

                    JENNY
          I scratch their eyes out.

                    TONY
          Yikes.

                    JENNY
          That's why I keep these long nails.

(Jenny holds out her nails)

                    TONY
          What's painted on them?

                    JENNY
          Pokemon characters.

(Tony takes her hands in his and looks at them)

                    TONY
          Cool.

                    JENNY
          Not really, but I like them.

(Tony still holds her hands)

                    JENNY (CONT.)
          You can let go now.

(Tony lets go of her hands)

                        TONY
          Sorry.

                        JENNY
          Tony?

                        TONY
          Yeah?

                        JENNY
          I know you like me.

                        TONY
          What? No! I mean... we're just
          friends right?

                        JENNY
          You like me more than that don't
          you?

                        TONY
          Why? Uh... that okay? I mean...

                        JENNY
          Tony... you're very nice. I enjoy
          being your friend and hanging out,
          but I feel like I'm leading you on
          or something. I just want to make
          things clear...

                        TONY
          Clear? How clear?

                        JENNY
          Pretty clear. I like someone
          else... that isn't you.

                        TONY
          Oh.

                        JENNY
          I'm really sorry... I don't want to
          hurt you, but giving you false hope
          isn't good either. The right woman
          will come along for you. I know it.

                        TONY
          I hope you're right.

                        JENNY
          She's out there. I really believe
          everyone has their soul
          mate. Their perfect match.

                                        (CONTINUED)

                    TONY
          Okay.

                    JENNY
          Please don't be upset, Tony.

                    TONY
          I'm fine. Don't worry about me. I
          gotta go, okay? See you later.

                    JENNY
          This is your home, Tony. I can
          go. See you later.

(Jenny exits and Tony sits sadly. Frank comes out)

                    FRANK
          Where's Jenny?

                    TONY
          She left.

                    FRANK
          What's with you?

                    TONY
          I'm not feeling good.

                    FRANK
          Something happen?

                    TONY
          Yeah... Jenny dumped me.

                    FRANK
          What? I didn't know you were even
          dating.

                    TONY
          We weren't... she just made it
          clear we never would.

                    FRANK
          Did she say why?

                    TONY
          She said she likes someone else.

                    FRANK
          Really? I wonder who?

                    TONY
          It doesn't matter. You know how
          long I've been trying to get a date
          with her?

                    FRANK
          Ever since we met her.

                    TONY
          I really thought I could wear her
          down.

                    FRANK
          Geez, man. That's not the best
          approach.

                    TONY
          It's usually what I do. Bug them
          until they want to kill me or give
          in so I shut up about it.

                    FRANK
          How many dates have you gotten from
          this approach?

                    TONY
          At least one.

                    FRANK
          Wow.

                    TONY
          You're no Don Juan yourself. How
          many dates have you had?

                    FRANK
          You don't have to get mad, Tony.
          I'm just trying to help.

                    TONY
          Well, it's not helping. You know as
          much about women as I do. We're all
          losers. We'll never get anyone and
          we'll all end up being stuck here
          together with Jenny around to
          constantly remind us how big of
          losers we are.

(Tony leaves the room and slams his bedroom door)

                    FRANK
             Yikes.

(Jenny re-enters cautiously)

                                              (CONTINUED)

                    JENNY
          Tony gone?

                    FRANK
          In his room.

                    JENNY
          Is he upset?

                    FRANK
          Yup.

                    JENNY
          Pretty mad at me?

                    FRANK
          At everyone. I made him pretty mad
          too.

                    JENNY
          Really? Why?

                    FRANK
          I tried to give him some advice but
          it's the blind leading the blind.
          I'm no lady killer.

                    JENNY
          You really haven't dated that much?

                    FRANK
          Not really. Maybe more than Tony
          and Randy, but not much.

                    JENNY
          Maybe I should give you all some
          tips.

                    FRANK
          I doubt it would help.

                    JENNY
          Don't get all emo on me.

                    FRANK
          Why not? Emo guys probably get
          more chicks than nerds.

                    JENNY
          Emo guys are so...
          depressing. Nerds are way more
          fun.

                         FRANK
          Yeah, we're just a barrel of
          laughs.

                         JENNY
          Tony really got you down, huh?

                         FRANK
          Yeah... I tried to be a friend but
          I just made him angry.

                         JENNY
          You meant well.

                         FRANK
          I am just trying to help. Why
          can't people see that?

                         JENNY
          This is really bugging you isn't
          it?

                         FRANK
          I know it doesn't seem like it, but
          I really care about all of you. I
          don't want to see any of you get
          hurt.

                         JENNY
          All of us? Me too?

                         FRANK
          Especially you.

                         JENNY
          Really?

                         FRANK
          You're... you're different than the
          guys...

                         JENNY
          I've noticed.

                         FRANK
          I mean Tony and Randy... they can
          be idiots... you... you're...

                         JENNY
          Not an idiot?

(CONTINUED)

                    FRANK
          No... I mean yes. It's just
          that...

                    JENNY
          What?

                    FRANK
          I don't know how to say this... I
          never know how to say anything
          right.

(JENNY sits him down)

                    JENNY
          Wait... wait... just stop and take
          a deep breath.

(JENNY holds his hands and FRANK takes a deep breath)

                    FRANK
          Deep breath.

                    JENNY
          Take your time. We're not in a
          hurry. And I'll listen to you.

                    FRANK
          You're like the only one. Everyone
          always talks over me or ignores me
          or changes the subject. Am I that
          boring?

                    JENNY
          Not to all.

                    FRANK
          What's interesting about me?

                    JENNY
          I love the way you joke about
          movies when we watch them. You
          make them twice as funny and twice
          as good. You can turn a horrible
          movie in to a giggle fest.

                    FRANK
          You like that?

                    JENNY
          We all do. That's why everyone
          wants to watch stuff with you.

                                              (CONTINUED)

                    FRANK
          I never thought about it before. I
          just like saying obnoxious things.
          I just assumed I was being rude.

                    JENNY
          Yes, but in the funniest way.

                    FRANK
          So that's what's interesting about
          me?

                    JENNY
          And music... I'm amazed at
          everything you know about music.

                    FRANK
          I just remember facts easily.

                    JENNY
          You know so much about so many
          songs and bands. I love listening
          to you talk old music.

                    FRANK
          New music sucks. I know nothing
          about 21st century music.

                    JENNY
          You're a good cook, a good
          leader... you keep these slobs in
          order... and you're a wonderful
          friend. You're loyal and would do
          anything for those who are
          important to you.

                    FRANK
          Wow, you actually make me sound
          like a decent person.

                    JENNY
          More than decent. Pretty awesome.

(They have a shy, awkward silence. Frank finally speaks)

                    FRANK
          Uh... Jenny?

                    JENNY
          Yeah?

                    FRANK
          Tony said you liked someone.

                    JENNY
          Uh-huh. A lot.

                    FRANK
          Who do you like?

                    JENNY
          You, Frank.

                    FRANK
          Really?

                    JENNY
          You're the reason I hang out here.

                    FRANK
          Geez... how did I miss that?

                    JENNY
          I was worried you'd never notice.

                    FRANK
          Why didn't you say anything?

                    JENNY
          A girl likes to be asked.

(She gets all aloof)

                    FRANK
          Jenny... would you like to go on a
          date with me... to the movies?

                    JENNY
          Yes! And pick a bad one. Let's find
          a single digit rating on Rotten
          Tomatoes.

                    FRANK
          And you really like my cooking?

                    JENNY
          I do.

                    FRANK
          I just follow the directions on the
          box.

                         JENNY
              You do it so well.

                         FRANK
              Then I'll whip you up a feast after
              our date too.

                         JENNY
              Make something we can sneak in to
              the theatre.

                         FRANK
              What? We can't do that. We'll get
              in trouble.

                         JENNY
              Come on. Live a little. Breaking
              the rules turns me on.

                         FRANK
              Let's see what we have in the
              kitchen.

(Randy enters)

                         RANDY
              Hey, I've done it again.

                         FRANK
              You clogged the toilet again?

                         RANDY
              No, better. I decided to embrace
              the whole video thing and use it to
              promote my start-up. I'm doing my
              own Kickstarter thing. I'm going to
              raise enough money to be a
              superhero like Batman. His
              millions bought him all kinds of
              cool stuff. My Kickstarter will
              too. Batman doesn't have any
              powers just like me.

                         FRANK
              Yes, you and Batman have so much in
              common.

                         RANDY
              I only need the money then I'm
              totally going hero.

Jenny gives him a dollar.

(CONTINUED)

                         JENNY
               Here you go, Randy. You're first
               dollar.

                         RANDY
               This is so awesome. Thanks Jenny.

(Randy runs off with his dollar all excited)

                         FRANK
               Don't encourage him.

                         JENNY
               But it's so cute.

                         FRANK
               Randy is not cute.

                         JENNY
               Jealous?

                         FRANK
               No.

                         JENNY
               Maybe a little?

                         FRANK
               Maybe.

                         JENNY
               Don't worry. No one is cuter than
               you.

                         FRANK
               Really?

                         JENNY
               Yeah... well, except for William
               Shatner.

                         FRANK
               True.

ACT III

(Act III is a street scene with three businesses: one with a
sign that says only PP, another that is a comic book store
and a third called "Macho Taco")

SCENE 9 - FIGHT THE MACHINE

(A woman, the Jane, is protesting outside a building with a
"PP" on the wall)

(A man, the TONY, approaches with a bag of computer
stuff. He can have a shirt with the business name like
"Computer Cowboys" or some such dorky name. She steps in his
way when he approaches. He tries to counter and she
counters)

                    TONY
          Um... I... uh... have to go...

                    JANE
          Go PP?

                    TONY
          No... uh... inside.

                    JANE
          No one is going inside.

                    TONY
          Why not?

                    JANE
          I'm protesting this place. What
          they are doing in there is wrong?

                    TONY
          Really?

                    JANE
          Yeah... don't you read the news?

                    TONY
          Sometimes... I have this app on my
          phone, but I never seem to know
          anything but celebrity news. I
          know all about upcoming movies and
          such... but I miss out on stuff
          like earthquakes and plagues and
          such. I really need a new app.

                    JANE
          Definitely.

                    TONY
          But I'm not a client. I just am
          here to fix their computers.

                                        (CONTINUED)

                    JANE
          I can't allow that either. If I
          stop their computers, then I stop
          them.

                    TONY
          Well, I don't know if the computer
          system will cripple them...
          although it seems like everything
          needs a computer these days. Even
          things like plumbing... even the
          plumbers are getting these little
          gadgets that you sign to pay the
          bill. I never like to touch plumber
          stuff though so it's really hard to
          sign it.

                    JANE
          So I stop you... then I stop them.

                    TONY
          I guess... kind of.

                    JANE
          So... stop.

                    TONY
          I'm stopping... now what?

                    JANE
          I'm not sure... no one ever stops.

                    TONY
          So they just kind of push past you?

                    JANE
          They say mean things usually and I
          get discouraged.

                    TONY
          Really? People can be such jerks
          sometimes.

                    JANE
          They won't even listen... at least
          they could take one of my brochures
          and keep an open mind.

                    TONY
          I'll take one.

                    JANE
          Really?

                    TONY
          Sure.

(Jane gets excited and gives him a brochure)

                    TONY (CONT.)
          Oh wow...

                    JANE
          What?

                    TONY
          This is the coolest looking
          brochure I've ever seen. I mean
          look at this artwork. Who did
          this?

                    JANE
          I did... each one is hand drawn...
          a unique piece of art from my soul.

(Tony looks at more than one)

                    TONY
          You're really good.

(Jane is embarrassed)

                    JANE
          Stop looking at my art and read
          what it's about... look at what
          this place is doing.

                    TONY
          That is kind of bad.

                    JANE
          Kind of? More than kind of.

                    TONY
          I didn't know they did this kind of
          thing.

                    JANE
          Doesn't it matter to you who you're
          helping?

                    TONY
          I just do my job... I don't really
          think about what a business might
                    (MORE)

                    TONY (cont'd)
          be doing... what they're mission
          is.

                    JANE
          It doesn't bother you that you're
          helping a place do something bad
          like this? Or you one of these
          people who think this isn't bad?

                    TONY
          I agree... it's bad... I've always
          thought so... I'm one of those
          people who think hurting any living
          thing is wrong... I'm anti-anything
          that harms the living... people or
          animals.

                    JANE
          You're all right, man.

                    TONY
          Thanks.

                    JANE
          Peace.

                    TONY
          Peace.

                    JANE
          You might be the first person I've
          stopped... and enlightened. How
          does it feel?

                    TONY
          Huh?

                    JANE
          To be enlightened?

                    TONY
          Not sure... kind of confusing.

                    JANE
          Talk to me about it.

                    TONY
          Uh... really?

                    JANE
          Yeah.

                         TONY
          Well... I have a job to do... but
          now I don't want to do it... and
          I'm wondering if I'll get fired if
          I don't.

                         JANE
          Oh, man... that's heavy.

                         TONY
          You've really embraced the hippy
          thing huh?

                         JANE
          Darn tootin.'

                         TONY
          But you're younger than me. And
          I'm not old enough to be a hippy.

                         JANE
          You're never too young to be a
          hippy... well, a flower child...
          I'm not in to the drugs and free
          love thing.

                         TONY
          Why not? I mean... that's good...
          I mean... drugs are bad.

                         JANE
          Free love ain't good either... love
          shouldn't be free for the taking by
          anyone. It should be about finding
          that perfect person... that single
          soul mate in this universe you were
          made for.

                         TONY
          Oh, so you mean like one person you
          love... not lots of people.

                         JANE
          Exactly.

                         TONY
          That would be nice.

                         JANE
          What?

                    TONY
          Finding that person.

                    JANE
          Yeah... finding that perfect
          match... the one who will be the
          yin to your yang... the balance to
          your force.

                    TONY
          Oh... Star Wars? You a fan?

                    JANE
          I've seen it enough... my brothers
          watched it over and over so many
          times I have it memorized.

                    TONY
          I'm a bit of a sci fi nut myself.

                    JANE
          You're a computer guy... I kind of
          figured.

                    TONY
          A guess that is a bit cliche'. And
          I supposed you like the movie the
          "Notebook"...

                    JANE
          What's cliche' about the Notebook?

                    TONY
          Seems like chicks always like the
          Notebook.

                    JANE
          That's not true.

(She gets annoyed and turns away, crossing her arms)

                    TONY
          I was just joking.

                    JANE
          Oh.

                    TONY
          Well... I guess I better go back to
          work and get fired or something.

(He starts to go slowly)

                         JANE
               Oh, man. I don't want you to get
               fired.

                         TONY
               But you're right. They are doing
               bad stuff in there.

                         JANE
               But I don't want you to lose your
               job. I'd feel terrible.

                         TONY
               It's okay... I hate my job. I
               never wanted to be computer guy.

                         JANE
               What do you want to be?

                         TONY
               A writer.

                         JANE
               What kind?

                         TONY
               I write sci fi... and superhero
               stories. I know... cliche'.

                         JANE
               I kind of like superhero stuff
               actually.

                         TONY
               Really?

                         JANE
               Who's your favorite hero?

                         TONY
               Oddly it's one no one ever heard
               of... but I have every comic... I
               loved the series... it's called
               ROM... it's about a robot alien who
               comes to earth to save humanity
               from these creatures that possess
               them. But he's all misunderstood
               and such because people think he's
               hurting people by destroying the
               alien demons inside them.

                          JANE
          Wow, that sounds cool. I've never
          heard of him before.

                          TONY
          Hardly anyone has. But I want to
          write something that cool... I want
          my work to have something to say...
          even if not a lot of people read
          it... I still want to say something
          good... and important.

                          JANE
          Right on, man.

                          TONY
          Who's your favorite superhero?

                          JANE
          I hate to say... yours is way
          cooler.

                          TONY
          Come on... tell me... I'm curious.

                          JANE
          I know everyone likes them but
          X-Men... I can't get enough of the
          X-Men. I especially like Rogue...
          I like how she can touch people and
          take their powers.

(Jane grabs Tony's hand. He is startled but doesn't pull
away. He likes it)

                          TONY
          I thought Rogue's touch could
          destroy a person.

(She looks at him)

                          JANE
          You look okay... feel okay?

                          TONY
          I feel a little funny.

                          JANE
          Don't die on me now.

(She hugs his hand and then lets go)

                                              (CONTINUED)

                    JANE
          Did I steal any of your powers?

                    TONY
          I'm not sure... know anything about
          computers?

                    JANE
          Not more than before. And I already
          play most those games you know.

                    TONY
          What makes you think I am a gamer?

                    JANE
          Don't all guys like you play video
          games?

                    TONY
          Guys like me?

                    JANE
          Cute computer guys?

                    TONY
          Cute?

                    JANE
          Yeah, you're kind of cute.

                    TONY
          Oh...

                    JANE
          You didn't know that you're cute?

                    TONY
          Well... uh... I didn't... I mean...
          I don't think...

                    JANE
          Geez... you just got cuter.

                    TONY
          Stop that.

                    JANE
          I can't call you cute?

                    TONY
          Not... here...

                          JANE
          Where?

                          TONY
          I don't know.

                          JANE
          You're blushing.

(She takes his hand. He looks around nervously)

                          JANE (CONT.)
          Does holding your hand make you
          nervous?

                          TONY
          I don't know.

                          JANE
          Want me to stop?

                          TONY
          I don't know.

                          JANE
          Geez... stop being so cute.

                          TONY
          Okay.

(She looks at his hands)

                          JANE
          So what games have you played?

                          TONY
          Nothing recent... except Angry
          Birds.

                          JANE
          Everyone has played Angry Birds.

                          TONY
          Angry Birds Star Wars.

                          JANE
          Okay... not that one.

                          TONY
          I'm from the old school of
          gaming... I've even played Pong. I
          love arcade games... going to the
          arcade with a bag of
                          (MORE)

                         TONY (cont'd)
          quarters. Something about standing
          there... losing tons of quarters...
          seeing how long you could make a
          quarter last. Quarters made it
          exciting... made it a challenge...
          made you play harder... and I loved
          watching people play too... I would
          have had fun watching you play.

                         JANE
          Watching me? That's creepy.

                         TONY
          I'm sorry.

                         JANE
          Creepy in a cute sort of way.

                         TONY
          Don't you think that's true
          though... that playing at home is
          missing something... it's so much
          cooler playing when people can see
          you do it... like a performance
          art... and it's a community...
          arcades were a community for people
          like me.

                         JANE
          Like us... I liked them too. I'm
          just old enough to see them die
          out.

                         TONY
          I still hunt around for arcades...
          stuck in corners of bowling alleys
          and pizza places.

                         JANE
          Pizza and video games... a match
          made in heaven.

                         TONY
          Oh, yeah... you're telling me.

(They smile at each other shyly and then are quiet. She
moves closer to him and holds his hand again)

                         JANE
          So... what you gonna do?

                    TONY
          Actually... I could take down their
          entire computer system.

                    JANE
          Really?

                    TONY
          I could plant a virus... one that
          would clear their entire system...
          all their client lists... all their
          schedules and appointments.

                    JANE
          That could shut them down... not
          forever but it's a start. I'd love
          you forever if you did that.

                    TONY
          Oh... well... I... uh...

                    JANE
          Do it... please.

                    TONY
          I've never done anything bad like
          this before.

                    JANE
          It's not bad... it's good... really
          good. What they do is bad. So very
          very bad.

                    TONY
          My first act of social protest...

                    JANE
          Making a difference.

                    TONY
          Fighting the machine.

                    JANE
          Fight the machine, man.

                    TONY
          I'll make it look like I fixed
          everything and then tonight the
          virus can kick in. Even if they
          don't trace it back to me, I still
          might get fired... but I don't
          really care anymore. It would be a
          blessing in disguise. I have some
                    (MORE)

                        TONY (cont'd)
            savings... I could write for
            awhile. Maybe I could do a
            comic... you could illustrate...
            you're good.

                        JANE
            Not that good.

                        TONY
            Best artist I've ever met.

                        JANE
            How many artists have you met?

                        TONY
            A few.

                        JANE
            Liar.

                        TONY
            So... should I do it?

                        JANE
            Yes... please... and we're go have
            pizza after... I know a place that
            has these video games in the
            tables.

                        TONY
            I love those... it's a date... I
            mean... it's a...

(She takes his hands again)

                        JANE
            It's a date.

                        TONY
            Okay.

                        JANE
            Go get 'em... make me proud, cutie.

                        TONY
            Fight the machine.

(She gives him a kiss on the cheek)

                        JANE
            For good luck... for a good man.

                         TONY
          Am I good?

                         JANE
          The best.

                         TONY
          Here goes.

                         JANE
          You're a hero today... fighting for
          life.

                         TONY
          May the living triumph over the
          machine.

                         JANE
          Yeah, man!

(He goes inside)

                         JANE (CONT.)
          Groovy.

SCENE 10 - MY WILLIAM SHATNER MAN CRUSH

(Spotlight)

                         FRANK
          Why am I waiting in line with all
          these losers? I am a grown man...
          With a job... I don't even live in
          my parents basement. Yet here I
          am... Waiting in line to meet
          William Shatner. I even got here
          early. I have a sleeping bag...
          Snacks... I am not even going to
          explain about the bathroom
          situation. Why do we put ourselves
          through this? I have dignity... I
          have a life... I don't need this. I
          should walk on out of here and
          leave this insanity behind me.
          Shatner once told us to get a life.
          It's time I got one.

(Then he gets excited when he sees William Shatner approach)

                         FRANK (CONT.)
          There he is!

(Frank squeals with excitement)

                                         (CONTINUED)

                              FRANK (CONT.)
                    He's coming over here! William
                    "frackin'" Shatner is coming over
                    here to meet me.

(Frank looks at a person who is in front of him)

                              FRANK (CONT.)
                    Oh, wow, Mr. Shatner. This is such
                    an honor... Yes sir... First in
                    line to see you. You're my favorite
                    celebrity. Well, my favorite person
                    in the whole world actually. I love
                    everything you've done. Everything
                    is better when you're in it. I love
                    Star Trek, T.J. Hooker, 3rd Rock
                    from the Sun, Miss Congeniality,
                    Boson Legal... even the Priceline
                    commercials... I love you...
                    Meeting you is the most magical
                    moment in my life so far... Thank
                    you, Mr. Shatner... Call you Bill?
                    Oh wow... Bill. Bye bye... Live
                    long and stay awesome!

(Gets really embarrassed and disgusted with himself)

                              FRANK (CONT.)
                    Oh my God! What is wrong with me?!
                    What am I? A fan girl? I need my
                    head checked... Oh, no... I have a
                    man crush, don't I? I have a
                    William Shatner man crush. I want
                    to die now. Crawl under a rock with
                    the other creepy fans... And....

(He notices they are opening the doors at the store he is
waiting in line at)

                              FRANK (CONT.)
                    They're opening the doors! I am so
                    getting my boots autographed.

(Frank picks up a bag with something in it)

                              FRANK (CONT.)
                    Hey Bill! Look why I found on eBay
                    for you to sign! It's the actual
                    rocket boots from Star Trek V!

(Jenny runs up)

                         JENNY
          Thanks for holding my place in
          line. So we really gonna meet the
          Shat?

(People in line behind them [can be other actors off stage]
start complaining)

                         PERSON 1
          Hey!

                         PERSON 2
          What gives?

                         PERSON 3
          No cuts!

(Jenny grabs on to Frank)

                         JENNY
          Quit your whining. This is my
          boyfriend. And if you nerds are
          good I'll let you watch me kiss
          him.

(Jenny acts like she is going to kiss Frank but he resists)

                         FRANK
          Jenny. Stop.

                         PERSON 1
          Well...

                         PERSON 2
          I don't know.

                         PERSON 3
          You have a girlfriend?

                         PERSON 1
          I guess...

                         PERSON 2
          If I had a girlfriend, I'd let her
          take cuts.

                         PERSON 3
          I don't know.

                         JENNY
          How about I let you take a picture
          of me kissing William Shatner?

                        FRANK
          What?! Jenny!

(They all cheer)

                        ALL
          Yeah!

                        JENNY
          Let's go boys!

(Jenny takes Frank by the hand and leads him off)

SCENE 11 - MUNCH MY MACHO TACO

(Randy is in his wrestling mask and has a sign that says
"Munch my Macho Taco." He has a sign dancing job where he
stands on street corner with an advertising sign - a dream
job for him. An old lady, Sadie, is watching him and
checking him out)

(Randy does a silly dance with his sign and sings to the
tune of Macho Man by the Village People)

                        RANDY
          "Hey, hey, hey, hey, hey! Macho,
          Macho Taco. I wanna eat a Macho
          Taco." Hey!

(Sadie pinches Randy on the butt)

                        RANDY
          I told you not to bother me while
          I'm working, Sadie.

(Sadie giggles and wanders off. Randy goes back to waving
his sign)

                        RANDY
          It's a tough life... Being a
          celebrity. But I am a star now. My
          fans demand I dance.

(Randy shakes his booty at the audience)

                        RANDY
          Maybe I should insure my booty like
          JLo... Cause when I shake this
          thang it's gold. Macho taco said
          their sales are way up since I
          started this. They sold like 10
          extra tacos yesterday. They almost
                        (MORE)

                                              (CONTINUED)

                          RANDY (cont'd)
                    ran out of tortillas. I can't
                    believe I get paid to do this. This
                    is like a dream job for me. I mean
                    this is what I do anyway. When I
                    home alone, I crank up the music
                    and dance!

(Randy does a silly dance move)

                          RANDY
                    Except at home I usually ain't
                    wearing nothing but my undies.

                          SADIE
                    I'd pay to see that! You wear them
                    tidy whities just like Tom
                    Cruise? You wanna show me your
                    Risky Business.

                          RANDY
                    The hard part about this is all the
                    fans. Ever had groupies? It's
                    crazy. I mean I don't mind the
                    drive by fans who shout out things.
                    They're cool.

(Randy points to passing car and tries a Hulk Hogan
impression)

                          RANDY
                    "Eat a macho taco, brother!" But
                    it's the creepy ones that hang
                    around and watch you... and wanna
                    touch you.

(Sadie pinches him again)

                          RANDY (CONT.)
                    Knock it off, Sadie. Don't damage
                    the merchandise. I gotta keep
                    working this baby.

(Does Mr. T impression to passing car)

                          RANDY (CONT.)
                    "I pity the fool who don't eat no
                    Macho Tacos."

(Randy dances and Sadie tries to join in)

                              SADIE
                    Yeah! Shake it! Like the San
                    Francisco quake of 19 ought six.

                              RANDY
                    Chicks think this job is hot.

(Randy does a cowboy dance like he is on a horse)

                              SADIE
                    Ride 'em cowboy!

(Sings to tune of "Mony Mony" by Billy Idol)

                              RANDY
                    "So good! Macho taco! So good!
                    Macho taco! Come on! Come on!"

(Sadie and Randy dance as lights go down)

                         END OF PLAY

Printed in Great Britain
by Amazon